TABLE OF CONTENTS

01	THE BIRTH OF A WORRYWART
02	THE ART OF OVERTHINKING
03	PANIC ATTACKS: MY FRENEMIES
04	THE JOYS OF SOCIAL ANXIETY
05	GOOGLING SYMPTOMS: A TALE OF TERROR
06	THE SLEEP-OVERTHINK CYCLE
07	SELF-CARE FOR THE OVER-CAFFEINATED
08	TRAVELING WHILE ANXIOUS: A COMEDY OF ERRORS
09	THE ART OF SAYING NO (WITHOUT OVER-EXPLAINING)
10	THRIVING, ONE DAY AT A TIME

Introdution

Anxiety is normal but there's levels.

My name is Asim and I suffer from anxiety, there I said it !! this feels like a AA meeting. So yes I'm 50 years old and have been suffering for nearly 35 years with anxiety. With this book I have tried to add some humour to this serious issue that affects around 301 Million people around the world, nearly 4% of mankind and hope to help people and give them hope and let them know you can still live a beautiful and happy life no matter how bad you feel at times, and some tips on how to deal with situations you may be in with anxiety.

I'm here to give hope and laughter at the same time.

THE BIRTH OF A WORRYWART

You ever wake up in the middle of the night and think, "Did I turn the stove off?" only to realize you haven't used the stove in three days? Congratulations—you might be a worrywart, like me! And let me tell you, it's not something that happens overnight. Oh no, it's a finely tuned skill honed over years of unnecessary panic and totally avoidable catastrophizing. If anxiety is an art, I'm basically the Picasso of freaking out over nothing.

Let me take you back to the beginning: The Birth of a Worrywart.

It all started when I was a kid. Back then, I was pretty carefree, running around, collecting bruises, and convincing myself that eating dirt was a completely legitimate snack option. Life was good! But then something happened. My parents, God bless them, did what all well-meaning parents do—they tried to protect me from the world. They warned me about hot stoves, busy streets, and the lurking danger of "stranger danger," which, as a child, I assumed meant every person I didn't know was basically a ninja with bad intentions.

Suddenly, I started to look at life a little differently. There was a whole world of things to worry about that I hadn't even considered! "What if I accidentally step on a crack and break my mom's back?" became a daily dilemma. I started walking like a human pretzel to avoid sidewalk cracks. And don't even get me started on the time I read that a spider could crawl into your mouth while you sleep. To this day, I sleep with my mouth clamped shut like a determined clam, just in case.

As I grew older, my worrying graduated from stepping on cracks to the more sophisticated, adult fears: "Did I leave the iron on?" "Am I forgetting something crucial?" "What if I get trapped in an elevator with a mime?" (A valid fear, if you ask me.)

I started to notice that my mind had a special talent for taking normal situations and turning them into potential crises. For example, a simple knock on the door isn't just a knock. Oh no, it's clearly the FBI. Or the IRS. Or worse—someone trying to sell me something, and I'll feel too awkward to say no, so now I own 12 boxes of overpriced candles. Even when it's just the neighbor asking for some sugar, my heart's already in overdrive, planning an escape route like I'm in an action movie.

The real kicker, though, came during middle school. Ah, middle school, the breeding ground for all kinds of insecurities. My anxiety found its wings here, soaring to new heights. A pop quiz? My palms would sweat like I was on a game show, and the stakes were life or death. A school dance? You mean a room full of people waiting to see me trip on my own feet and become the laughingstock of the century? (Spoiler alert: I did trip, but no one cared because everyone was too busy freaking out about themselves. A lesson I learned way too late.)

But the crowning jewel of my anxiety education came when I got my first job in high school. I was a cashier at a grocery store, which, for most people, is a pretty straightforward gig. For me, it was a battlefield of potential disasters.

"What if I accidentally charge someone twice?" I'd think as I swiped items across the scanner, hands shaking as if I was defusing a bomb. "What if someone gives me a counterfeit bill and I get arrested for fraud? Is that even how it works? Oh God, am I going to jail?!"

My manager once caught me double-checking the same customer's total for the fifth time and asked, "Are you okay?" To which I responded, "Of course! I just have a healthy sense of paranoia." He gave me a puzzled look, probably deciding whether I needed therapy or a vacation, and walked away slowly.

And let's not forget the joys of technology. You'd think the invention of email and texting would make communication easier, right? Not for me! Whenever I send an email, my anxiety shifts into overdrive. What if I accidentally sent it to the wrong person? Or worse, what if I accidentally hit "Reply All" and now everyone in the company knows about my questionable lunch choices?

I've spent entire afternoons re-reading emails for typos like they were going to be engraved in stone for future generations to see. "Did I sign off with 'Best' or 'Thanks'? Oh no, did 'Thanks' sound passive-aggressive? Should I have added a smiley face? No, wait—that's too casual. They'll think I'm unprofessional!"

And text messages? Don't even get me started on the read receipts. They are the absolute bane of my existence. There's nothing quite like sending a message, watching the little bubble pop up as the person reads it, and then... nothing. Silence. My heart starts racing, and my brain takes over, filling the void with all sorts of worst-case scenarios.

"They hate me."
"They're mad at me."
"They've been kidnapped by international spies mid-text."

Of course, they're probably just busy, but that's not where my mind goes first. My brain skips the logical explanation and heads straight for the plot of a suspense thriller.

The birth of a worrywart isn't one event. It's a series of tiny, seemingly insignificant moments that build up over time until one day you realize that you've become the person who packs extra underwear for a two-hour car trip, just in case.

My friends often joke that I'm the human embodiment of a "What if?" scenario. I have a talent for imagining the most bizarre, unlikely outcomes. Like, "What if I'm eating soup and I accidentally sneeze, and the soup goes up my nose, and then I choke, and no one's around to save me, and I die because of soup?" Totally reasonable, right?

Over time, I've come to accept my role as the resident worrywart. It's not that I enjoy being anxious—it's just that my brain likes to stay prepared. You know, for everything. And while it can be exhausting to constantly live in a state of "what if," I've learned to laugh at myself along the way. Because if you can't laugh at your own ridiculousness, then you'll probably cry—and crying is just one more thing to worry about.

So here I am, fully embracing my title as a professional worrywart. And if you ever need someone to help you overthink every possible scenario of your life choices, I'm your person. Just don't ask me to make any decisions—I'll need at least three days, a pro-con list, and probably a Google search on how to not regret everything forever.

The Art of Overthinking

If overthinking were an Olympic sport, I'd be a gold medalist, standing proudly on the podium, nervously wondering if the national anthem sounds a little off-key or if my shoelaces are tied unevenly. You see, overthinking isn't just a habit for me—it's an art form. A finely tuned skill that I've mastered over the years, capable of turning the most mundane situation into a full-blown mental thriller.

Overthinking is like having an overactive brain that's obsessed with plot twists. Take something simple, like sending a text. A normal person might shoot off a message without a second thought. But me? Oh no, I'll spend twenty minutes crafting it, another ten analyzing it, and the next hour worrying about whether or not it conveyed exactly what I meant.

Imagine this: I text a friend, "Hey! What time are we meeting later?" Simple, right? Except as soon as I hit send, my brain starts dissecting it like it's an unsolved crime. "Wait, did the exclamation mark seem too enthusiastic? Should I have used a period instead? Oh God, what if they think I'm annoyed because I didn't add an emoji? Is 'later' too vague? What if they think I'm being passive-aggressive?!"

Before you know it, I'm spiraling. Should I send a follow-up message to clarify? But then, what if that makes it worse? What if they see two messages and think I'm desperate for validation? By the time I've finished obsessing over the text, my friend has already replied with a casual "6 pm ●." Mystery solved, but not before my brain made it a detective noir with dramatic voiceovers and everything.

The thing about overthinking is it doesn't care if you're dealing with big life decisions or if you're just trying to pick out a sandwich at a deli. The deli scenario is a classic. I step up to the counter, and the pressure is on. The guy behind the counter is staring at me, waiting, and suddenly, I'm paralyzed. Should I get the turkey sandwich? Or maybe the tuna salad? But what if the turkey's dry? What if the tuna has too much mayo? Should I ask for extra pickles, or will that make me seem high-maintenance? And what if I make the wrong choice and spend the rest of the day regretting my lunch decision?

It's at this point that the deli guy raises his eyebrows, as if to say, "Come on, it's just a sandwich." But no, sir, it is not just a sandwich. It's the potential for a food-related existential crisis. After all, one wrong sandwich could ruin my entire day. I finally blurt out, "I'll take a salad," which wasn't even an option I was considering but now seems like the safest, least-judged choice. Of course, I'll spend the next two hours wondering why I didn't just stick with the turkey.

One of the prime breeding grounds for overthinking is the workplace. Ah yes, the professional setting, where overthinking really gets to flex its muscles. Let's say my boss sends an email that says, "Can we chat later?" That's it. No details, no context. You know what that means, right? I'm getting fired. It doesn't matter that I've been doing a good job, meeting all my deadlines, and not setting the building on fire—my brain immediately goes into worst-case scenario mode. "What did I do? Did I forget to reply to an email? Did I say something weird in the last meeting? Is this about that awkward joke I made by the coffee machine?"

And then the real fun begins. I start mentally preparing for every possible outcome. Maybe my boss just wants to ask a quick question. Or maybe I'm about to be dragged into a three-hour meeting about how my coffee breaks are too long. Or—my personal favorite—I'm secretly under investigation for some bizarre office crime I didn't even know existed, like improper use of office supplies.

The meeting comes, and my boss simply asks if I can help with a new project. Easy, no drama. But by then, I've already spent half my workday planning my apology speech, updating my résumé, and imagining a future where I live off-grid in a cabin, away from the horrors of professional email misinterpretation.

Public speaking is another goldmine for overthinking. Let's say I'm asked to give a presentation at work. I spend days meticulously preparing every word, every slide, every pause for dramatic effect. But when the big moment arrives, I'm suddenly hyper-aware of every possible thing that could go wrong. What if I trip on the way to the podium? What if my slides don't load? What if I accidentally say something wildly inappropriate, like calling my boss "Mom"? (Don't ask why this is a recurring fear, but it is.)

Then comes the post-presentation overthinking. Did I talk too fast? Did I make enough eye contact? Was my joke about Excel spreadsheets funny, or did everyone just politely chuckle out of pity? By the time I'm done dissecting every second of my performance, I've convinced myself I bombed it so badly that I'll be remembered as the person who ruined PowerPoint for everyone, forever.

Overthinking isn't limited to the big stuff, either. It loves to worm its way into everyday life. Like when you're lying in bed at night, ready to drift off into a peaceful sleep, and suddenly—BAM! Your brain goes, "Hey, remember that time in 2008 when you waved back at someone who wasn't waving at you? Yeah, let's think about that for the next two hours."

Overthinking turns me into a human time machine, transporting me back to every awkward interaction, every cringeworthy moment, every time I mispronounced a word in front of someone important. And then, just for fun, my brain likes to toss in some completely irrational scenarios. "What if I accidentally sent an email to my entire contact list with nothing but the word 'potato' in it?" Or "What if I wake up tomorrow and completely forget how to tie my shoes?" You know, the usual stuff.

My personal favourite overthinking moment has to be when I buy something online. I'll spend hours researching the best version of whatever I'm buying. Say it's a toaster. I'll compare prices, read reviews, watch YouTube videos of people toasting things. (Yes, those exist.) Finally, I'll make my purchase. But as soon as I hit 'buy,' the doubt creeps in. Did I pick the right one? Should I have gone for the one with the bagel setting? What if it doesn't fit on my counter? And then I spend the next three days refreshing the tracking page like a hawk, worrying that the toaster will arrive broken or, worse, not toast evenly.

Here's the thing about overthinking: it's exhausting. It's like carrying around a full suitcase for a trip you're not even going on. But the upside? I've learned that overthinking has a strange sense of humor. It's kind of like living with a dramatic, over-caffeinated inner monologue that just can't take a break. Sure, it turns everything into a production, but at least I'm never bored.

So, whether it's deciding what to have for lunch, interpreting a one-word text, or bracing myself for some imaginary disaster, I've accepted that overthinking is just part of who I am. Maybe it's not the most efficient way to live, but it sure does keep things interesting. And who knows? One day, all this overthinking might actually come in handy. Like when I'm preparing for the apocalypse... or just trying to figure out what to wear to a wedding.

But until then, I'll be here, second-guessing whether I used the right amount of exclamation points in that email and wondering if I left the stove on. (I didn't, but I'll probably check again—just in case.)

Panic Attacks: My Frenemies

Ah, panic attacks. Those unexpected, uninvited guests who crash the party of life like they're the star of a chaotic reality show. They come in, make a dramatic entrance, flip over the metaphorical coffee table of your emotions, and then leave you wondering what just happened. If I had a dollar for every time I had a panic attack, I could afford a lifetime supply of those weird stress balls that never actually seem to help.

You see, panic attacks and I, we go way back. We're like frenemies—always lurking, always ready to make my life interesting at the most inconvenient times. It's like having a hyperactive, overzealous friend who just loves to shout, "SURPRISE!" when you're trying to mind your own business, sipping coffee, or, I don't know, existing peacefully.

But let's rewind. My relationship with panic attacks began, as all great relationships do, in the most unexpected way possible. I was sitting in a movie theatre, enjoying my popcorn and watching an animated film about talking animals. Life was good. I had no major worries—other than whether I'd finish my popcorn too soon and be left snack less for the rest of the movie. Then, out of nowhere, my heart started racing, my chest tightened, and my hands got clammy. What is this? I thought, suddenly convinced that my body had decided to have a full-blown emergency right there in front of animated squirrels.

My first instinct was the obvious one: I was dying. Right there in the middle of a kids' movie. A literal disaster. I clutched my popcorn as though it contained some kind of life-saving serum and waited for the sweet release of death—or at least for the usher to bring me smelling salts (do ushers even carry those?).

Except, of course, I wasn't dying. This was my very first panic attack, and it had chosen to debut during a G-rated film. Not exactly the dramatic setting I would've picked for a near-death experience, but hey, panic attacks don't care about your aesthetic. They just want to make an entrance, and boy, do they know how to do that.

When I eventually calmed down—after the credits rolled and I convinced myself I didn't need to be carried out on a stretcher—I started Googling my symptoms. Which, by the way, is a terrible idea. "Heart racing, sweating, dizziness" was immediately diagnosed by the internet as everything from "mild dehydration" to "about to meet your maker." Very helpful, thanks WebMD.

It wasn't until I visited an actual doctor that I learned the truth: "You had a panic attack," she said, as casually as if she were telling me I'd caught a cold. "It's not uncommon." Oh, great. So not only did I not have some rare, exotic disease, but I now had to accept that my brain could just hijack my body at any moment like a rogue pilot?

The worst part about panic attacks? They're unpredictable. You can't schedule them like a dentist appointment. No, they show up whenever they please—usually when you're minding your own business, like standing in line at the grocery store or trying to make small talk at a party. "Hey there, long time no see," they seem to say as they stroll in, heart-pounding and palms sweating, uninvited as always.

Here's a fun example: I was once in the middle of a perfectly ordinary work meeting. The kind where everyone is pretending to listen but is really thinking about what they'll have for lunch. I was nodding along like a pro, contributing exactly nothing of value, when BAM! Panic attack time! My heart started racing, and my brain decided that it was the perfect moment to freak out over the fact that, technically, I was just sitting in a chair and breathing—but what if I was doing that wrong?

Suddenly, the idea of sitting became terrifying. "Is this what sitting is supposed to feel like? Am I too tense? Do I look calm? Is everyone else in the room noticing how weirdly I'm sitting? What if I forget how to sit entirely and fall off the chair?!" Of course, I didn't fall off the chair, but I did start wondering if this was how I'd meet my professional demise—crumbling into a panic puddle while my boss discussed sales projections.

But panic attacks aren't just limited to sitting in chairs and watching harmless movies. Oh no. Sometimes they strike at moments that should be fun. Picture this: you're on vacation, lounging by the pool, sipping a fruity drink with an umbrella in it. The sun is shining, the breeze is perfect, and you should be having the time of your life. And then—wham!—a panic attack decides this is the ideal moment to kick in. Because nothing says "relaxation" like suddenly wondering if you're about to drown in three feet of water while holding a piña colada.

.

It's in these moments that my brain goes full conspiracy theorist, spiraling into scenarios that are so far-fetched even Hollywood would be like, "Okay, that's a bit much." My mind becomes a rapid-fire game of "what if?" What if I can't breathe? What if I faint? What if I actually get sucked into a black hole of anxiety and no one ever finds me again?

I've also developed a bizarre panic attack radar. You know, like a weather forecast but for freakouts. I'll wake up and think, "Today feels like a good day for a panic attack." Sure enough, it'll hit me when I'm doing something completely innocent, like brushing my teeth or folding laundry. Folding laundry! How is that stressful? I'm not in a high-stakes folding competition, but suddenly, my brain goes, "YOU FOLDED THAT SHIRT WRONG. EVERYTHING IS WRONG!" And boom—instant panic.

It gets to the point where I start analyzing every tiny physical sensation like a detective hunting for clues. "Is my heart beating too fast? Is it normal to feel a little dizzy when you stand up? Did I just blink weirdly? Does that mean I'm about to faint?" My brain takes these tiny, normal bodily sensations and amplifies them like I'm living inside a medical drama. It's like my inner hypochondriac and panic attack conspire to keep me on my toes. They're like, "She thinks she's fine. Let's remind her she's never fine."

Of course, after a while, I started to realize that panic attacks, while absolutely terrifying, are also kind of ridiculous in hindsight. I mean, let's be real here—I wasn't going to die because I folded a shirt poorly or waved back at someone who wasn't actually waving at me. But try telling that to my brain in the middle of a panic spiral. My brain isn't into logic. It's into drama. My brain loves drama.

And so, I've come to accept panic attacks as my strange, inconvenient companions. We don't always get along, but I've learned to deal with them. I've even developed some coping strategies. Deep breathing? Sure. Counting backward from 100? I'll give it a go. Telling myself that literally no one has ever fainted from folding laundry? Works about half the time.

But the best strategy? Laughing at the absurdity of it all. Because, honestly, if I didn't laugh at how ridiculous my brain can be, I'd probably spend all my time curled up in a blanket fort, hiding from imaginary crises. Which, come to think of it, doesn't sound that bad, but that's a different story.

So, here's to my panic attacks, my frenemies. They may make me feel like I'm riding a rollercoaster without a seatbelt, but at least they keep life interesting. And if you ever find me mid-panic in a random location—like the grocery store or a petting zoo—just give me a reassuring nod and maybe a snack. We'll get through this, one absurd freakout at a time.

The Joys of Social Anxiety

Social anxiety is like that awkward party guest who shows up uninvited and proceeds to make everything weird. You know, the kind of guest who stands in the corner, obsessively overthinking how they said "hello" and wondering if their handshake was too firm, too limp, or, somehow, both at the same time. That's social anxiety in a nutshell: the constant fear that you've done something irreparably awkward and everyone's judging you for it—when, in reality, they've already forgotten you even said anything.

Let's be clear: I didn't choose social anxiety. It chose me. It's like a personal assistant I never hired, constantly whispering in my ear, "Don't say that," "You're probably annoying them," and "Why did you just wave at someone when they were clearly waving at the person behind you?" Social anxiety is a funhouse mirror version of life where every interaction is distorted, awkward, and vaguely horrifying.

Take small talk, for example. To a normal person, small talk is just a pleasant way to fill silence. For me, it's a gladiatorial death match of words. You can almost hear the announcer's voice in my head: "Ladies and gentlemen, in the left corner, we have a friendly acquaintance who's just trying to ask how your weekend was. And in the right corner, it's me—terrified, overthinking every syllable, and about to respond with something wildly inappropriate like 'Oh, you know, just counting the days until I ruin my life!'"

The pressure of small talk turns my brain into a word salad generator. A simple "How are you?" can make my mind go completely blank or, worse, prompt a panic-stricken monologue that overshares my latest existential crisis. "How am I? Oh, well, I'm great! Except for that weird pain in my back which I'm pretty sure is nothing but could also be a rare condition. But other than that, fine! Totally fine! How are you?" All while my inner voice is screaming, "Abort! Abort! You've already said too much!"

And don't get me started on group conversations. You know those people who just effortlessly glide into a conversation and say something funny or insightful? Yeah, I'm not one of those people. I'm the one lurking on the fringes of the conversation, mentally rehearsing what I might say—if I ever get a chance to jump in, which I won't, because by the time I've perfected my witty comment, the conversation has moved on to a completely different topic, and now I look like I'm about to burst out with a fact about bread in the middle of a discussion about global politics.

Then there's the dreaded moment when everyone turns to you for your input. I don't care if they're asking me my opinion on world peace or whether I prefer cats or dogs —the sudden spotlight makes my brain short-circuit. "Uh, yeah, I think… um… dogs are… good? Yes. Dogs are good. They have… fur." Nailed it. Meanwhile, inside, I'm screaming at myself: Why didn't you just say literally anything else?

Social anxiety also makes exiting conversations a high-stakes mission. How do normal people just leave? They say something like, "I've got to get going," and then, poof! They're off to live their best lives. Not me. I approach every exit like I'm sneaking out of a hostage situation. I wait for a lull in the conversation, which never comes, and then when I finally get the courage to excuse myself, it comes out as this weird, abrupt, "Okaythanksbye!" followed by a nervous shuffle backward like I'm moonwalking out of the room. Smooth.

Don't even mention public speaking. A normal person might get butterflies in their stomach before giving a speech. I get an entire colony of bats. If I'm asked to speak in front of a group, I spend the days leading up to it rehearsing what I'm going to say. I practice it so many times in front of the mirror that I start to wonder if I've somehow forgotten how to form words. By the time I get up there, I'm convinced that I'll either accidentally speak in another language or just burst into song. Because that's where my brain goes—straight to the worst-case scenario.

My personal favorite (read: most hated) social anxiety situation? Parties. Oh, parties. They are a special kind of torture designed specifically for people like me. The invitation alone sends my brain into overdrive. Do I go? Do I decline? If I decline, will they think I'm avoiding them? But if I go, will I spend the entire time hovering awkwardly near the snack table, clutching a drink like it's a life preserver?

Let's say I decide to go. I'll arrive at the party (ten minutes early, because being late would be social suicide), and immediately my brain starts analyzing every detail. "Are you smiling too much? Not enough? Why did you pick that shirt? Is it weird that you said 'hi' twice to the same person? Is it weirder if you don't say 'hi' again and they think you're ignoring them? Quick, make a joke! No, not that joke!"

And then, of course, I'll say something completely bizarre, like, "I really like the color of this ceiling. Very… beige." Now the host is staring at me like I've just insulted their entire life, and I'm planning my exit strategy before I've even finished my drink. Spoiler: the exit will not be graceful.

Let's not forget the joys of phone calls. Oh, the panic that sets in when your phone rings and it's not a scheduled, premeditated conversation. I will stare at the screen like it's a ticking time bomb. Do I answer? What if I stutter? What if they ask me something I don't know the answer to? What if I pick up and it's just breathing sounds? By the time I've worked through this mental crisis, the call has gone to voicemail, and now I'm left with the equally terrifying task of having to call back. Social anxiety has officially turned me into someone who dreads hearing the phone ring, like a Victorian noblewoman afraid of modern technology.

Speaking of modern technology, let's talk about texting, shall we? Texting should be a safe space for the socially anxious—it's written communication, after all. No pressure to respond in real time. And yet, somehow, it's become another battlefield of awkwardness. I will spend an eternity crafting the perfect response to a text, then stare at it for ten more minutes, second-guessing every punctuation mark.

Did I use too many exclamation points? Does "Sure!" sound too aggressive? Should I throw in an emoji to soften it? But which one? The smiley face feels passive-aggressive, the winky face is just plain weird, and the thumbs-up might make them think I'm being sarcastic. Oh no, now I've waited too long to reply and they'll think I'm ghosting them! Send! SEND!

Of course, as soon as I hit send, the post-text panic sets in. Did I say too much? Too little? What if they don't reply at all? Now I'm refreshing my messages like it's an Olympic sport, analyzing every second that goes by without a response. It's been five minutes, and they still haven't replied. Should I send a follow-up? What if they did reply, but the message got lost in cyberspace, and now they think I'm ignoring them?

And that's how a simple conversation about where to meet for lunch turns into a full-blown psychological thriller.

Social media is no better. Don't even get me started on the horrors of posting something online. I'll compose a tweet, stare at it for 20 minutes, and then decide it's not funny enough to justify the potential embarrassment. On the rare occasion that I do post something, I immediately regret it. Within seconds, my brain starts its post-posting spiral. Why did I say that? Was that an appropriate use of hashtags? Oh God, people are going to think I'm trying too hard.

The funny thing about social anxiety is that it makes you think the whole world is watching your every move. In reality, no one cares that much. Everyone is too busy worrying about their own stuff to notice that you said "you too" to the waiter when he told you to enjoy your meal. But try telling that to my brain in the middle of a social anxiety flare-up. My brain doesn't care about logic or facts. It's too busy crafting a narrative where I'm a socially awkward disaster that people will talk about for years.

Here's the thing: social anxiety might be a daily challenge, but it's also kind of funny when you look at it from the outside. I mean, who else gets to experience the pure adrenaline rush of saying "hello" to a stranger like it's a life-or-death situation? Who else rehearses their food order in their head 17 times before actually saying it out loud to the waiter?

Sure, social anxiety makes me overthink every interaction, but it also gives me some great stories. Like the time I over-apologized to a cashier because I thought I handed her the wrong amount of change (I didn't). Or the time I waved at someone in the grocery store and then spent the next hour hiding in the cereal aisle because I wasn't sure if they were waving at me or someone else. (They were waving at someone else. I'm still cringing about it.)

So, while social anxiety may not be the most fun guest at the party, it's definitely the most memorable. We may never fully get along, but at least it keeps life interesting—and, when all else fails, I've learned to laugh at the absurdity of it all. Because really, what else can you do when your brain turns "ordering a coffee" into an Olympic-level mental challenge?

Googling Symptoms: A Tale of Terror

Let me start by saying, I'm not a doctor, but thanks to the internet, I now think I am. And not just any doctor—a specialist in every field, from cardiology to obscure tropical diseases I've only ever heard of because I googled "random rash on hand." Yes, my journey into the world of digital self-diagnosis is nothing short of a horror story— a tale of terror that starts with a simple sneeze and ends with me writing my will in the middle of the night.

Now, you'd think with all of modern medicine at our fingertips, Googling your symptoms would be reassuring. "It's just a cold," you'll tell yourself. "I'll just check online, you know, to confirm that I'm fine." Spoiler alert: You're never fine. Because, as any seasoned WebMD enthusiast knows, the moment you enter your symptoms into that search bar, you've essentially clicked "Start" on a game of Worst Case Scenario Roulette.

Let's talk about the gateway drug to health anxiety: the headache. Everyone gets headaches. But as soon as I get one, my brain immediately jumps to, "What if it's a brain tumor?" And then, like the overachiever I am, I decide to confirm my fears by Googling "headache, left side, slightly worse after coffee." Up pops a list of possible causes. The first one? "Caffeine withdrawal." The second one? "Stress." But the third one, just waiting there, hiding behind the more reasonable explanations like a horror movie villain in the shadows? Brain-eating amoeba.

Boom. I'm done for. My normal, everyday headache has just escalated from "maybe too much screen time" to "the countdown has begun, and there's nothing anyone can do."

The thing about Googling symptoms is that it doesn't matter if 99% of the results say you're fine. That 1% of terrifying, worst-case outcomes? That's all you need to send yourself into a full-blown spiral of dread. I've spent more time in online symptom checkers than some doctors spend in med school. I should probably be awarded an honorary degree for the sheer amount of medical research I've (mis)interpreted.

Let's move on to another personal favorite: the random body ache. One day, I'm minding my own business, watching TV, when I notice a weird twinge in my leg. Do I stretch? Maybe drink some water and call it a day? Of course not. I open my laptop like I'm about to crack the Da Vinci Code and type "dull pain in right leg while sitting." Now, in a rational world, I'd get a result like "poor posture" or "muscle cramp." But no. Instead, I'm met with "deep vein thrombosis" or—better yet—"rare, unnamed nerve disorder only diagnosed twice in history, one of which was on the moon."

The escalation happens so fast it's almost comical. I start with a reasonable thought—"Maybe I've been sitting too long?"—and within five minutes, I've convinced myself that my leg is one day away from full amputation. Suddenly, I'm Googling prosthetic limbs and preparing myself for life as a one-legged motivational speaker. This is not an exaggeration. This is how my brain works when mixed with the dangerous cocktail of a vague symptom and unlimited internet access.

The throat tickle is another one. You're sitting there, minding your own business, when your throat feels… funny.
Nothing major, just a tiny scratch. But that's all it takes. "It's probably allergies," I whisper to myself, already pulling out my phone and typing "throat feels weird for no reason." The results? "Common cold" followed immediately by "throat cancer" and "rare parasitic infection that only occurs when you accidentally swallow contaminated water while scuba diving in a remote part of the Amazon rainforest." (Note: I've never been scuba diving.)

Of course, after reading this, I'm now thoroughly convinced that I've developed some kind of hyper-rare illness, despite my absolute lack of exposure to the Amazon, parasites, or even adventurous water sports. Suddenly, I'm chugging tea with honey and obsessively checking my reflection to see if my neck looks swollen. I even start mentally preparing for the call to my doctor, which I'm sure will go something like this:

Me: "I'm calling because I think I have a rare parasitic throat infection." Doctor: "Have you recently been in the Amazon rainforest?" Me: "No, but I Googled it, and the symptoms match!"

By this point, the doctor is already mentally preparing to prescribe a calming tea, because what I actually have is not a deadly disease, but a case of extreme hypochondria. I'll realize this too, eventually —about five hours later when my throat is fine and I'm embarrassed I nearly declared it a national health emergency.

for me. In a normal world, a rash is likely to be caused by something like an allergy, heat, or maybe just sensitive skin. But not in my world. Oh no. In my world, that tiny red bump is definitely a symptom of some ultra-rare, unpronounceable disease, probably one that was last seen in medieval Europe.

The first result is always something simple, like "dermatitis" or "allergic reaction to soap." But then I scroll a bit, because I'm nothing if not thorough, and I find myself in the deep, dark corners of the internet where things like "flesh-eating bacteria" lurk. Suddenly, my innocent little rash has transformed into a ticking time bomb, and I'm looking at images of skin conditions that no human should ever Google. Why do I do this to myself?

I've learned that no matter how calm I am when I start, I will inevitably leave the experience convinced that I am either one sneeze away from full-blown disaster or the subject of a future medical mystery on "House."

Once, I had a harmless twitch in my eye. Nothing dramatic, just a little flutter that happens sometimes when you're tired. Naturally, I hopped onto Google and typed "eye twitching on left side, normal?" The first response? "Stress." Okay, that seemed fair. But, of course, I kept scrolling, and there it was: "Could be a sign of a neurological disorder." Great! Within minutes, I had convinced myself that this was the beginning of some slow, irreversible decline. My eye was twitching, and soon, I'd probably lose all motor control. That's it. My life as a functioning adult was over.
Spoiler: It was just stress.

And let's not even start on the rabbit hole of all my symptoms at once. You know, the moments where you have a headache, a mild cough, and maybe an ache in your back, and you're like, "Hey, why not enter all these into Google at the same time? What could possibly go wrong?" Everything. Everything could go wrong.

Because instead of getting a result like "You're probably just tired, chill out," the internet will piece together your symptoms like some kind of medical detective and announce, "Based on your input, you might be experiencing an incredibly rare combination of diseases that nobody has ever survived. Good luck!"

The worst part? I know how irrational this all is. Every time I find myself staring at the screen, reading about some tropical disease that I have a 0% chance of contracting, I tell myself, "You're fine. Stop Googling." But can I stop? Of course not. At this point, it's like a bad habit—a strange compulsion to confirm my worst fears, despite the overwhelming evidence that I'm just overreacting to perfectly normal human sensations.

There are moments, though, where I triumph. I'll feel a weird ache or notice something minor, and instead of Googling, I'll say, "You're okay. This is normal. You don't need to go down that rabbit hole." And for about five minutes, I'll bask in the glory of my newfound self-control. Until, inevitably, the thought creeps back in. But what if you're wrong?

And then, before I know it, I'm back on WebMD, diagnosing myself with a condition so obscure, even the internet barely has any information on it. "Looks like I'll be the first case study," I think to myself, while simultaneously opening tabs on rare diseases and holistic treatments. It's a vicious cycle.

But hey, at least I've learned a lot about obscure medical conditions. I might not be qualified to perform surgery, but I can definitely tell you about the dangers of Googling "random muscle twitch" at 3 a.m. So, if you ever need advice on how to transform a paper cut into a life-or-death situation using only an internet search engine, I'm your girl. But, for the love of all things healthy, don't ever follow my lead.

My biggest takeaway from this terrifying tale? There are two types of people in the world: those who trust their doctor, and those who think Google knows better.

I, unfortunately, belong to the latter group. And while I'm not proud of it, I can at least laugh at the fact that I've spent more time diagnosing imaginary conditions than actual doctors spend diagnosing real ones.

So here's to Google, the enabler of my deepest medical fears. May we one day part ways, but until then, I'll be over here, Googling "why does my nose feel slightly cold when I eat ice cream."

The Sleep-Overthink Cycle

Sleep, they say, is supposed to be a peaceful, restorative time. You know, that blissful part of the day when your body recharges, your mind rests, and you drift off into a dreamland where all your problems melt away. Well, for most people, that's true. For me? Not so much. Because when my head hits the pillow, it's not the start of sleep—it's the start of The Sleep-Overthink Cycle, a nightmarish loop where I'm trapped between my bed and my brain, unable to escape the overthinking vortex.
Let me walk you through it.

Step 1: The Illusion of Calmness
It always starts out so innocently. I'm tired. I've had a long day. I'm ready to sleep. I brush my teeth, I change into my pajamas, and I slide into bed like a normal human being who intends to close their eyes and drift off into sweet, uninterrupted slumber.

For the first few minutes, things seem hopeful. The room is dark, the bed is comfy, and for a moment, I think, Tonight is the night I'll sleep like a regular person. I take a deep breath, get comfortable, and close my eyes. There's a brief, fleeting moment of calm, where I foolishly believe I might actually fall asleep without any mental gymnastics.

Step 2:

The Intrusive Thought
Just when I'm teetering on the edge of dreamland, a rogue thought sneaks in. It's always something random and mildly unsettling, like: "Did you lock the front door?" Suddenly, I'm wide awake, eyes open, staring at the ceiling.

I probably did lock the door. I always lock the door. I'm sure of it. Except, what if tonight's the one night I didn't? What if I got distracted? What if someone breaks in? What if, in the morning, the police are standing over me, shaking their heads like, "You should've checked the door, buddy."

So now, of course, I have to get up and check. I drag myself out of bed, trudge to the door, and—surprise!—it's locked. Just like it always is. So I go back to bed, feeling slightly foolish but satisfied that at least I've addressed the issue.
Except now, I'm awake.

Step 3:

The Rabbit Hole of Regret

At this point, my brain decides that since we're already awake, it's a good time to review my entire day, month, or maybe even my whole life. You know, just to make sure I've fully cataloged every awkward moment, every embarrassing thing I've ever said, and every mistake I've made since kindergarten.

It'll start small. "Hey, remember that email you sent earlier? Did it sound passive-aggressive? Maybe you should've added an extra exclamation mark. Or a smiley face. Wait, what if your boss thinks you're angry? Maybe you should send a follow-up right now."

I try to argue with my brain. It's 1 a.m. No one sends follow-up emails at 1 a.m. Also, the email was fine. But my brain is not convinced. "Was it, though? What if they're talking about it right now? Maybe they're having a secret meeting about how weird your email was. What if tomorrow they ask you to explain it?" Now, I'm sweating. That email is definitely going to come up in my performance review.

Just when I think I've settled that anxiety, another thought pops up: "Hey, remember that thing you said to your friend three weeks ago? You know, that joke that didn't land? What if they've been secretly mad at you this whole time? What if that's why they didn't text you back right away last Thursday?"

Great. Now I'm spiralling about a conversation I barely remember and planning my apology speech for something that might not have even offended anyone.

Step 4:

Overthinking About Overthinking

At this point, I start worrying about the fact that I'm worrying. My inner voice becomes increasingly exasperated: "Why are you like this? Just go to sleep. People fall asleep all the time. It's a natural process! Why are you incapable of doing the one thing that babies and dogs are better at than you?"

Which, of course, only makes things worse. Because now, instead of relaxing, I'm stressing out about how much time I'm wasting by not relaxing. "If you fall asleep right now, you'll still get six hours of sleep. That's totally fine! Just close your eyes and… WAIT, now it's 5 hours and 47 minutes. Come on! You're wasting time!"

There's a countdown happening in my brain, and it feels like I'm about to miss a critical deadline: The deadline to fall asleep. But the harder I try, the more awake I feel. Sleep has become the prize I'm chasing, and my brain is running interference like it's getting paid to sabotage me.

Step 5:

Existential Crisis O'Clock
Somewhere between 2 a.m. and 3 a.m., I hit the jackpot: existential dread. Because why stop at overthinking my email or the door lock when I can zoom out and question the very fabric of my existence?

"Why are we here?" my brain muses. "What's the meaning of life? What if nothing really matters, and everything you've done so far is just a random blip in an indifferent universe?"

Okay, brain, I get it—you went to Philosophy 101. But now? Right now? Is this the ideal time to be pondering the mysteries of existence? Can we save this for the shower tomorrow morning, maybe?

But nope, there I am, lying in the dark, staring at the ceiling, wondering if I've been wasting my life by not pursuing my true passion (whatever that may be) or if humanity is just doomed anyway, so why bother?

Step 6:

The Desperate Bargaining Phase
Around 4 a.m., I start negotiating with myself. "Okay, listen. If you fall asleep right now, you can still get four hours of sleep. Four hours is totally manageable. You'll be a little tired, but you'll survive. Just breathe. Relax. Don't think about how little sleep you're going to get. Definitely don't calculate the minutes. Just… let… go."

Spoiler alert: I do not, in fact, let go. Instead, I start trying to fall asleep, which is like trying to look cool when you're holding a massive plate of spaghetti—you're just destined to fail.

I'll roll over to my other side, adjust my pillow 37 times, kick my leg out from under the covers, and even try the "pretend to be asleep" method, which is essentially just lying there motionless while silently screaming in your head: "Why. Aren't. You. Asleep?"

Step 7:

The Sudden Burst of Productivity
Somewhere around 5 a.m., my brain decides that since sleep is a lost cause, it's time to get productive. This is when I get a sudden burst of energy and think, "Maybe I should just stay awake and get a head start on the day."

In a normal world, this might sound like a solid plan, but at 5 a.m., with three hours of overthinking under my belt, my logic is deeply flawed. I'm not going to write a best-selling novel or clean my entire apartment in the pre-dawn hours. I'm going to scroll through my phone, read random articles about productivity hacks (irony!), and maybe start reorganizing my sock drawer before I give up and flop back into bed.

But by this point, I'm too awake to sleep, and too tired to do anything useful. I'm stuck in limbo, a zombie drifting through the early morning, my brain buzzing with a hundred different thoughts while my body just wants to tap out.

Step 8:

The Inevitable Nap
Finally, just as the first light of day starts creeping through the window and the birds begin chirping, I feel the wave of sleepiness I've been chasing all night. My body, exhausted from fighting its own thoughts, starts to shut down. My eyes get heavy, my brain finally quiets down, and I drift off into... a 20-minute nap.

Yes, right as the alarm goes off, my body finally decides it's time to sleep. Classic.
I wake up feeling groggy, frustrated, and betrayed by my own brain. I shuffle through my morning routine like a sleep-deprived zombie, making myself coffee and vowing that tonight will be different. Tonight, I will not overthink myself into oblivion. I will not fall into the sleep-overthink cycle.

And then... 10 p.m. rolls around, I brush my teeth, get into bed, close my eyes—and it all starts again.
Because if there's one thing I can count on, it's that my brain is a night owl with a love for spirals, and I am forever trapped in the relentless cycle of overthinking my way through the night.

Self-Care for the Over-Caffeinated

Ah, coffee. The nectar of productivity. The elixir of life. The socially acceptable adult pacifier. Whether it's your first cup in the morning, your mid-afternoon pick-me-up, or that desperate, slightly shameful cup you down at 8 p.m. because deadlines wait for no one, coffee is always there for you—steady, reliable, and making your hands just a little too shaky to be trusted with anything delicate.

But let's face it: coffee, as much as it's the fuel that powers most of our daily decisions, is also the culprit behind many of our less stellar moments. Like, say, the time you drank an espresso at 5 p.m., only to find yourself reorganizing your closet at 3 a.m. while contemplating the meaning of life and wondering why your heart is auditioning for a drum solo in a heavy metal band.

Which brings us to the real issue: if you're over-caffeinated (which, let's be honest, you probably are), you need to engage in some serious self-care. Yes, self-care.

The thing you think you're doing when you drink a lavender latte, but actually you're just adding fuel to the jittery fire that is your nervous system.

So, buckle up, my fellow caffeine junkies. It's time to talk about how to practice self-care when you're already three cups deep and can't stop vibrating long enough to even consider decaf.

Step 1: Hydrate Like It's Your Job

After cup number three of coffee, I'm approximately 90% caffeine and 10% guilt. My mouth may taste like a burnt rubber band, and my eyelid might be twitching like it's getting paid by the twitch, but that's a small price to pay for alertness, right?

Wrong. As it turns out, you need actual water to function. I know, shocking. Every time I refill my coffee mug, I should technically be matching it with a glass of water. Do I do this? Of course not. But I've read about it, and that's almost the same thing.

Here's how this goes down: after realizing my over-caffeinated brain has hit the point of diminishing returns and my eyes are starting to feel like I'm squinting into the sun, I'll tell myself, "Hey, maybe you should hydrate." So I'll drink a glass of water like I'm trying to make up for the last 24 hours in one gulp. Instantly, my body is like, "Oh, hello! Are we finally taking care of ourselves?"

It's a great start. Except now I have to go to the bathroom approximately every six minutes because my kidneys are like, "You ignored us all day, now watch us work!"

So, yes—self-care tip number one: Drink water. It won't undo the fact that your body is currently trying to metabolize three double shots of espresso, but at least you'll feel like you're pretending to be healthy.

Step 2: Yoga for the Jittery

Yoga is supposed to be calming, right? A way to center yourself, connect with your breath, and just be. But when you're wired on caffeine, yoga turns into a test of how long you can hold downward dog without shaking like a Chihuahua in a snowstorm.

Picture this: I'm standing on my yoga mat, taking deep breaths, trying to focus on the calm, serene instructor on YouTube. She's all like, "Inhale deeply, feel the earth beneath your feet…" Meanwhile, I'm over here vibrating like I just snorted a line of powdered sugar.

My heart's racing, my leg is twitching, and instead of "feeling the earth," I'm feeling like I could outrun a cheetah—or have a heart attack mid-warrior pose.

I'm halfway through a sun salutation when I realize I've been holding my breath for the last 30 seconds because I'm so focused on not spilling the gallon of caffeine that seems to be sloshing around in my system. The instructor says, "Relax," but my brain hears, "It's a race! Faster!" and now I'm accidentally doing a cardio workout when I was supposed to be centering myself.

Yoga for the over-caffeinated is less about finding inner peace and more about not collapsing into a twitching pile of nerves. But hey, at least I'm moving, right?

Step 3: The Calm App (But on Fast-Forward)

Next, I try meditation. You know, the thing you're supposed to do when you feel stressed or overwhelmed—two feelings that, coincidentally, show up shortly after my third cup of coffee.

So I open up one of those meditation apps, ready to experience some serious zen.
The soft, soothing voice starts: "Close your eyes. Take a deep breath. In… and out…"
And already, I'm losing it.

My caffeinated brain is like, "In and out? Got it! Let's go! Inoutinoutinoutinoutinout…" and I'm hyperventilating instead of relaxing. The Calm App voice is telling me to picture a peaceful stream, but all I can think about is how I should've emailed my boss back at 2 p.m., or if I remembered to take the chicken out of the freezer, or why my left toe feels slightly weird right now.

Meanwhile, the meditation app is still droning on about "noticing the breath," but I'm too busy noticing the fact that I'm about to have a caffeine-induced existential crisis.
By the end of the session, I haven't achieved a state of calm—I've achieved a state of rapid-fire, caffeine-fueled brainstorming. I've solved three problems that didn't need solving and created four more.

Step 4: Snack Attack

Another key element of self-care? Eating real food. And no, by "real food" I don't mean a protein bar you found at the bottom of your bag or the three almonds you snacked on between meetings. I mean actual food that isn't powered by sugar and caffeine.

Here's the thing: after drinking a small ocean's worth of coffee, my stomach has officially gone on strike. It's like, "Nope, we're not digesting solid foods anymore, but we will accept more coffee if you have it."

But self-care means eating something, so I go for something sensible, like a salad. Except by the time I'm done staring at my greens, I've convinced myself that a salad just won't cut it. I need something that says, "I'm doing great," like a burger. Or pizza. Or ice cream. Anything that'll make up for the fact that I've basically been running on adrenaline and espresso fumes all day.

Self-care tip: eat something other than a liquid stimulant. Bonus points if it has actual nutrients and doesn't involve ordering from a drive-thru at midnight.

Step 5: The Art of Napping (Or Trying to, Anyway)

The pinnacle of self-care for the over-caffeinated is the nap—the elusive, mythical creature that promises to restore you to a state of calm and balance, if only for 20 minutes. The problem? Napping on caffeine is like trying to calm a toddler who's eaten an entire bag of Skittles.

I lie down, close my eyes, and immediately my brain is like, "Oh, you want to rest? Let's think about every decision you've made since high school! Also, here's an imaginary scenario where you accidentally ruin your best friend's wedding—have fun with that!"

Instead of falling asleep, I end up lying there, wide awake, with my heart racing and my mind playing a highlight reel of every embarrassing thing I've ever done. It's like my brain is in overdrive, and the idea of falling asleep feels like trying to lull a tornado to sleep with a lullaby.

Eventually, I give up on the nap and decide to just "rest my eyes," which basically means lying in bed, pretending I'm relaxed, but really just scrolling through my phone with one eye open.

Step 6: Accepting the Jitters

At some point, you just have to accept the fact that your body has officially gone rogue. You're jittery. You're on edge. You could power a small city with the amount of caffeine coursing through your veins. And that's okay. The sooner you accept that your over-caffeinated state is your fault, the sooner you can take some deep breaths (or attempt to, anyway) and move on.

Self-care, when you're over-caffeinated, isn't about completely calming down. It's about managing the chaos you've willingly created. Maybe you'll go for a walk, or take a bath, or just stare at the wall for 20 minutes while your brain replays that one awkward thing you said in 2008. But you'll survive. We always do.

So there you have it: a foolproof (okay, slightly flawed) guide to self-care when you've had too much coffee. It's not perfect, and you'll probably still end up with a case of the jitters and a mild existential crisis, but at least you'll be hydrated, stretched, and pretending to meditate while your brain races at 1,000 miles per hour.

And who knows? Maybe next time, you'll actually skip that fourth cup of coffee and go for something like herbal tea. Or, you know, maybe you'll just embrace the chaos and go for espresso shot number five.

Either way, self-care is a journey. A jittery, over-caffeinated, sometimes-shaky journey.

Traveling While Anxious: A Comedy of Errors

Ah, travel! The promise of adventure, the allure of new experiences, and the undeniable joy of seeing the world! For most people, this is the moment to get excited, pack bags, and embrace spontaneity. For me? Traveling is an exercise in preparing for every possible catastrophe, and my brain treats it like a high-stakes, world-saving mission where any wrong move could lead to a personal apocalypse.

Yes, welcome to the wonderful world of Traveling While Anxious, where every trip feels like a heist movie, except instead of stealing a priceless artifact, I'm just trying to survive a flight without crying in the airport bathroom.

Step 1: The Packing Paralysis

Packing, for most people, is a relatively straightforward task. They throw in a few outfits, some toiletries, and boom—they're good to go. But for me, packing is where the anxiety show really kicks off. It's not just about shoving clothes into a suitcase—it's about preparing for every single possible scenario, from a formal dinner on the beach (which I have not been invited to, nor ever will be) to a sudden outbreak of a zombie apocalypse.

Here's how it goes: I start with the basics—T-shirts, jeans, socks. Easy, right? Except then my brain kicks in. "Wait," it whispers, "What if it rains the entire time? Do you have an umbrella? How about a rain jacket? Better bring extra socks in case they get wet. Actually, better bring waterproof socks. Do those exist? You should Google that."
And we're off to the races.

Suddenly, I'm considering every possible weather pattern, googling "will it snow in Bali," and packing six pairs of shoes for a weekend trip. Will I need a bathing suit and a parka? No? Better pack them just in case.

The real kicker is the toiletries. I start out with the essentials—deodorant, toothpaste, shampoo. But my brain chimes in: "What if the hotel doesn't have soap? You should bring soap. Actually, bring two kinds of soap, one for your face and one for your body. Oh, and what if you need a first aid kit? And hand sanitizer? And allergy medication, even though you've never had an allergic reaction in your life? Better pack it, just in case."

By the end of this packing extravaganza, I've got enough supplies to last me through a small apocalypse and am wondering why my suitcase weighs more than me. Meanwhile, people who travel with just a backpack and one pair of shoes are like mythical creatures to me—possibly elves, maybe wizards. I don't know how they do it.

Step 2: The Airport Gauntlet

Arriving at the airport is where the real fun begins. For the average traveler, it's a minor inconvenience—take off your shoes, get through security, grab a coffee, and wait for your flight. For me, it's a full-on military operation.

The night before, I don't sleep. Not even a little bit. I'm too busy mentally preparing for all the ways I could accidentally miss my flight. What if there's traffic? What if I forget my ID? What if the plane leaves early just to mess with me? So, I arrive at the airport approximately five hours before my flight is scheduled, just to be safe.

I know—"you only need two hours before a flight." Amateurs. Two hours is a lie invented by laid-back people who haven't considered the fact that TSA might one day randomly decide you look suspicious because your shoes are too squeaky.

The minute I step into the airport, I'm in survival mode. First stop: the check-in counter. Even though I've checked in online, I still approach the desk like I'm smuggling a live ferret in my luggage. I hand over my ID with a shaky smile, convinced that at any moment, they'll look up and say, "Sorry, this isn't you. We have no record of your existence. You're actually a ghost. Please leave."

When that doesn't happen, I'm relieved for a nanosecond before heading to security. Ah, security—the part of the airport experience where every single traveler suddenly feels like they've committed a felony.

Despite having nothing even remotely illegal or suspicious on me, I panic. What if I accidentally brought a knife? Or a bomb? Or a giant tub of shampoo? I once got flagged for a granola bar, so now everything feels like a potential red flag.

I take off my shoes, my jacket, my belt, and place all my worldly possessions into those sad little plastic bins. The security agent says "Step through the scanner" in a tone that makes me feel like I'm about to enter The Hunger Games. And, of course, every time I step through, I somehow set off the alarm. Maybe it's my glasses. Maybe I'm just radiating stress. Who knows?

After a humiliating pat-down where I try to explain that I'm not harbouring any secret weapons in my pockets, I'm finally through security. But am I relieved? Oh, no. I'm now entering the gate anxiety stage.

Step 3: Gate Anxiety (aka: The Waiting Game)

Now, all I have to do is wait for my flight, which is easier said than done when you're convinced that your plane is going to leave without you, or worse, crash into a remote jungle where you'll have to survive on airline peanuts for the next 40 years.

So I arrive at the gate and sit down. Then I check the gate number again. And again. And again. Yes, I'm at Gate 23. I've checked the screen, the ticket, and the app. But what if they change it without telling me? I start eavesdropping on nearby conversations, trying to figure out if they know something I don't.

The second there's an announcement, I'm at full attention, waiting for them to say, "By the way, we're actually leaving from Gate 57 across the airport, and if you don't sprint, you'll miss it."

Then there's the boarding process itself. Every time they announce a new boarding group, my heart leaps. What if I miss my group? What if they skip my row? I'm practically hovering by the boarding line with my ticket clutched in my sweaty hand, like a nervous child waiting to be picked for dodgeball.

When they finally call my group, I rush onto the plane like I'm trying to escape a zombie horde. I get to my seat, buckle up, and then recheck my seat assignment three times, just to make sure I haven't stolen someone else's spot. Then I settle in and prepare for the next wave of anxiety.

Step 4: In-Flight Freakout

The flight itself is where the real magic happens. For most people, this is the time to relax, maybe watch a movie, take a nap, or enjoy some complimentary snacks. But for me? It's the time to consider every possible way the plane could malfunction.

The second we hit turbulence, my brain goes into full meltdown mode. The pilot comes over the speaker with a cheery, "We're just hitting a little bumpy weather," but all I hear is, "We're going down, folks. Hope you said your goodbyes."

At this point, I'm gripping the armrest like it's the only thing keeping me alive, mentally reciting every reassuring fact I've ever heard about air travel. "Planes are safe. You're more likely to get struck by lightning. This is normal." But my inner monologue just screams back, "TELL THAT TO THE TURBULENCE, ASIM."

Then there's the in-flight bathroom situation. I'm terrified of leaving my seat because the second I get up, I'm convinced the plane will hit a massive pocket of turbulence, throw me against the ceiling, and I'll end up sprawled in the aisle, covered in tiny pretzels.

So I stay seated, knees clenched, too scared to move for three hours, wondering if my bladder will hold out or if I'll just have to accept my fate as "the person who went viral for using a Ziploc bag as an emergency bathroom."

Step 5: The Arrival Anxiety (aka: Did My Luggage Make It?)

After surviving the flight (barely), I should be able to breathe a sigh of relief, right? Ha. No. Now we enter the final boss battle of travel: Baggage Claim.

As I stand there, watching the carousel go around, I feel a deep, existential dread settle in. What if my bag didn't make it? What if it's circling some airport in Iceland while I stand here, bagless, in Dubai?

One by one, people grab their bags and go, while I'm left waiting. And waiting. And waiting. By the time my suitcase finally appears, I'm half-convinced it's been lost forever, and I'm preparing to spend the rest of my life wearing airport gift shop T-shirts.

Step 6: The Anti-Climactic End

At long last, I stumble out of the airport, exhausted, mentally drained, and slightly paranoid that I forgot something important, like, I don't know—my entire identity. But I made it. I'm alive. I've survived the gauntlet of anxiety-fueled travel.

And now? Now I get to do it all over again for the trip back.

Traveling while anxious isn't a glamorous experience. It's not the carefree, Instagram-worthy adventure it's supposed to be. It's a never-ending spiral of worry, awkwardness, and heart palpitations that turn even the most basic trip into a full-blown production. But hey, at least it's never boring.

The Art of Saying No (Without Over-Explaining)

Saying "no" is supposed to be easy, right? Two little letters, one tiny syllable, and yet, for many of us, it's the verbal equivalent of climbing Mount Everest in flip-flops. You'd think I was being asked to deliver a soliloquy on the nature of existence, the way my brain spins out when someone makes a simple request.

The problem is, I don't just say "no." Oh, no. I launch into a full-blown press conference, where I explain in intricate detail why I'm saying no, how much I regret saying no, and how I'm a fundamentally flawed human being for even considering saying no in the first place.

This, my friends, is The Art of Saying No (Without Over-Explaining)—a masterclass in how not to accidentally sign up for a bake sale, a work project, or a weekend hike that you knew deep down you didn't want to do in the first place.

Step 1: The "Sure, I'll Do It" Reflex

Before we even get to the magical world of saying no, we need to address the reflex that causes many of us to just say "yes" to everything.

Someone asks, "Can you help with this project?" and before my brain even processes the question, my mouth is already saying, "Sure, I'd love to!" My brain, meanwhile, is screaming, "WHAT ARE YOU DOING? You don't have time! You don't even like spreadsheets! The last time you tried to work Excel, you accidentally created a pivot table that crashed your computer!"

But I say yes anyway, because I can't bear the thought of disappointing anyone. I can't be the person who says, "No, I'm busy." No, I have to be the person who says, "I'll help! And I'll bring snacks!" Why? Because, apparently, I have a pathological need to be liked by everyone—even that guy from accounting who thinks email chains from 2005 are still funny.

Step 2: The "No, But I Feel So Bad" Phenomenon

On the rare occasion that I do manage to summon the courage to say "no," things quickly spiral out of control.

Here's a real-life scenario: Someone invites me to a party. Now, every fiber of my being knows that I do not want to attend this party. The thought of making small talk with strangers while balancing a plate of questionable hors d'oeuvres is my personal nightmare. But still, I can't just say "no" like a normal person.

Instead, I say, "Oh, no, I can't make it, I'm so sorry, I have this thing with my family, you know, it's been planned for weeks, and I'd hate to cancel on them, but I really, really wish I could be there because your parties are always so fun, and honestly, I was looking forward to it, but then my dog has this thing with his paw, and I need to take him to the vet, and also I'm kind of coming down with something? So yeah… maybe next time?"

It's an Olympic-level verbal gymnastics routine, where I manage to guilt myself for saying no, over-explain every detail of my fake plans, and still leave the person wondering if I'm secretly avoiding them because they think I hate their cat (I don't! I just hate going places).

The worst part? By the end of this explanation, I'm so frazzled that I've basically talked myself into going to the party, after all. The person looks at me sympathetically and says, "Oh, I totally get it—feel better!" And now, I'm standing there wondering if I have to fake a cold or, worse, adopt a dog to keep up the lie.

Step 3: The Phantom Guilt

There's something that happens when you say "no," and it's called phantom guilt. This is the feeling that, by saying no, you've somehow committed a heinous crime against humanity. You haven't just declined an invitation; you've single-handedly destroyed someone's faith in humankind.

For example, say someone asks me to help them move this weekend. In a rare moment of clarity, I say, "No, I can't, I've got plans." I should feel good, right? Proud of myself for setting a boundary. But instead, I immediately spiral into a guilt vortex.

"Oh my god, I said no! What if they think I don't care about them? What if they're carrying a couch up four flights of stairs by themselves right now, silently cursing my name? I should have said yes. I could have said yes. I'm a terrible friend."

Before I know it, I've texted them back, saying, "Actually, if you really need help, I could come by after my plans! Or, you know, maybe before them! What time are you moving again? I'll bring donuts!"

In the end, I've not only agreed to help them move, but I've also volunteered to bring snacks and coffee, and somehow, I've made it all worse by first trying to say no. This is the Phantom Guilt at work—making sure that I turn a simple "no" into a full-blown disaster recovery mission.

Step 4: The Over-Explanation Trap

The core problem with saying no is my compulsive need to justify it. It's not enough for me to simply say, "No, thank you." I feel this overwhelming urge to give an acceptable reason, even though no one is actually asking for one. Because, deep down, I think, "If I don't explain, they'll think I'm a monster."

So, I explain. And I explain too much.
Imagine someone asks if I want to grab coffee. Simple question, right? If I'm not in the mood, I could say, "No, thanks, not today." But instead, I go down this rabbit hole: "No, I can't because I'm trying to cut back on caffeine, and actually, I'm doing this whole new sleep thing where I don't drink anything past 3 p.m., and also, I think I've developed an allergy to coffee beans, and my doctor told me I should try chamomile tea, and honestly, have you tried decaf? It's not the same. Anyway, so yeah, maybe next week?"

By the time I'm done, we've gone from a simple coffee invite to a TED Talk on caffeine's effects on the nervous system, and I'm pretty sure the other person has already fallen asleep.

Step 5: The Magical Power of a Simple No

Here's the truth I've had to come to terms with: saying no doesn't need an elaborate backstory. Most of the time, people aren't actually interested in why you're saying no—they just need to know whether or not to count you in. And yet, my anxious brain insists that every "no" is an invitation to an existential crisis.

But there's a magical power in a simple no. No explanation. No over-the-top reasoning. Just… "no." It's terrifying, but it works.

For example, imagine this scenario: someone asks me to join a group hike. In the past, I'd respond with something like, "Oh, I would love to, but my shoes aren't really good for hiking, and my ankle's been acting up, and I have this meeting later, and also, I'm a little scared of heights, and bugs, and the general concept of being outdoors, but thanks for asking!"

Now, though, I'm working on just saying, "No, I can't make it." No further details. No apologies. Just a simple, clean, clear "no."

And you know what happens? Nothing. No one throws a tantrum. No one demands an explanation. They just move on, find someone else to hike with, and life continues.

Step 6: The Aftermath

The first time I said "no" without over-explaining, I half-expected the sky to open up and rain fire upon me. But nothing happened. The world didn't end. The person didn't disown me as a friend. They just nodded and said, "Okay!"

And yet, for the next 48 hours, I still had to fight the urge to text them back with an in-depth apology and a pie chart showing exactly why I couldn't make it.

But over time, I've learned that saying no isn't the catastrophe I've made it out to be in my head. It's actually a form of self-care. It means I get to choose how I spend my time, without having to wriggle through an emotional maze of fake excuses and imagined guilt.

Saying no is a skill—one that requires practice, patience, and maybe a support group. But once you master it, you realize that it's not about being selfish. It's about being sane. Because, at the end of the day, no one needs to know that the reason I'm declining an invitation is that I plan to spend the evening in pajamas, rewatching a show I've already seen 12 times. That's my business. And the next time someone asks, "Hey, can you help with this thing?" I'll smile and say, with confidence:

"No, thank you."
And that'll be the end of it.

Thriving, One Day at a Time

Let's be real—when you hear the word "thriving," you probably picture a yoga-loving, green-juice-drinking, early-riser who posts motivational quotes like, "I'm not bossy, I'm the boss!" on Instagram. They're the type of person who wakes up at 5 a.m., journals their gratitude list, hits the gym, and still finds time to make an organic smoothie before heading to work.

Me? I wake up 20 minutes before I need to leave, wondering why I never, ever learn my lesson about hitting the snooze button 14 times. Thriving, in my world, means showing up to a meeting without coffee stains on my shirt and not forgetting that it's trash day. I may not be out here "crushing goals," but I've become a master at surviving and occasionally crushing a Netflix marathon. Baby steps.

This is what I like to call realistic thriving—a survival guide to taking life one day at a time when the closest you get to "self-improvement" is not losing your keys for the third time this week.

Step 1: Lowering the Bar (Because Sometimes, That's Thriving)

You know those people who say, "Shoot for the moon, and even if you miss, you'll land among the stars?" Yeah, I'm more of a "Shoot for getting out of bed before noon, and even if you miss, there's always tomorrow" type of person.

Here's the thing: thriving doesn't have to mean crushing it at work, running a marathon, or mastering the art of sourdough bread baking (seriously, why is everyone suddenly a baker?). For me, thriving means managing to get through a workday without using my phone as an emotional crutch or eating an entire sleeve of Oreos in one sitting (though let's be honest, sometimes that's still a win).

Lowering the bar isn't about settling; it's about being kind to yourself. You don't need to hit every milestone at 100 mph, you just need to hit the milestones that matter most to you—and some days, that milestone is as simple as folding laundry before it becomes a second wardrobe.

Step 2: The To-Do List of Realistic Expectations

Ah, the to-do list. The source of all motivation and the greatest source of crushing disappointment when you realize that "Write best-selling novel, clean entire house, learn Japanese" wasn't going to happen between the hours of 10 a.m. and 4 p.m.

I've come to realize that the key to thriving is creating a realistic to-do list. Forget the three-page bullet journal extravaganza that makes you feel productive just for writing it. No, I'm talking about the bare minimum. Because if we're being honest, most days, my to-do list looks like this:

1. Drink water (seriously, stop living off coffee).
2. Don't forget your keys.
3. Survive.
4. Maybe send that one email you've been putting off for six days.
5. Eat a vegetable (preferably one not shaped like a fry).

See? Manageable. And when I do cross something off? Victory dance. I've started to treat my to-do list like it's a game of Tetris: if I can make a couple of small pieces fit together by the end of the day, I feel like I'm winning. Sure, I didn't write that novel, but I did finally clean out the fridge, which is just as heroic in my world.

Step 3: Embracing the Power of "Good Enough"

There's a strange societal expectation that everything we do has to be perfect. Perfect job, perfect relationships, perfect Instagram-worthy brunches. But the secret to thriving—actually thriving—is embracing the power of "good enough."

Did I clean the house? Well, I vacuumed one room and hid all the clutter in the closet. Good enough. Did I cook a healthy dinner? Technically, I microwaved a frozen burrito, but it had beans in it, so I'm counting it. Did I work out? I stretched for five minutes this morning while trying to reach my phone that had fallen under the bed, so, yeah, that's movement.

I used to think I had to excel at everything to feel like I was thriving. Now I know that sometimes, just showing up is enough. Some days, you're a productivity machine, checking off boxes like a Type-A superhero. Other days, you're eating cereal for dinner while watching reruns of "The Office." Both days are valid. Both days can be thriving.

Step 4: Celebrating the Tiny Wins (Because Tiny Wins Add Up)

Here's the thing about thriving one day at a time: the little victories matter. Sure, you didn't revolutionize the world today, but did you avoid that third cup of coffee? Tiny win. Did you finally respond to that email? Tiny win. Did you refrain from doomscrolling before bed? Huge win.

I used to think success was about big moments—huge, life-changing achievements that you could post about with a #blessed hashtag. But now I realize it's the tiny wins that actually keep you going. Celebrating those tiny moments is what keeps the existential dread at bay. You don't need to wait for some epic achievement to feel good about yourself—just give yourself a high-five for putting on real pants today.

Step 5: The Art of Thriving in a World Obsessed with Hustling

We live in a society that glorifies hustle culture. Everywhere you look, there's someone telling you to "grind," "push harder," and "achieve greatness," as if your value as a human being is directly tied to how much you can accomplish before breakfast. I used to fall for it—thinking that if I wasn't constantly "hustling," I was failing.

But here's what I've learned: hustling doesn't equal happiness. In fact, hustling often equals burnout, anxiety, and a strong desire to move to a remote cabin with no Wi-Fi. Thriving, on the other hand, is about finding balance. It's about doing enough to feel fulfilled without pushing yourself to the brink of madness.

So instead of waking up at 5 a.m. to meditate, journal, and run a 5K before work, I've embraced a more laid-back approach to life. I wake up at a reasonable hour (okay, sometimes reasonable), take a deep breath, and tackle the day at my own pace.

I don't need to be a productivity machine 24/7. I can take breaks. I can have off days. I can binge-watch a whole season of a show and call it "self-care." Because guess what? That's thriving, too.

Step 6: One Day at a Time (Literally)

Thriving, at its core, is about being kind to yourself. It's about recognizing that not every day is going to be a home run. Some days, you're going to knock it out of the park, and other days, you'll barely make it to first base. Both days are okay.

The trick is to stop thinking about the long-term picture and focus on the day in front of you. It's easy to get overwhelmed when you think about all the things you should be doing. But if you take it one day at a time—one task at a time—it becomes more manageable. Instead of worrying about how you're going to finish that project by Friday, just focus on sending one email today. One small step. One small victory.

So when I say I'm thriving one day at a time, I mean it literally. Some days, thriving is about showing up for that meeting with a killer PowerPoint presentation. Other days, it's about surviving until 5 p.m. without spilling coffee on myself. Either way, I'm thriving, and that's all that matters.

Thriving isn't a one-size-fits-all concept. For some, it's about achieving big dreams. For others (like me), it's about making it through the day with minimal chaos. Either way, the goal is to find joy in the little moments and stop comparing yourself to those "perfect" people who seem to have it all figured out.

Because here's the truth: no one has it all figured out. We're all just winging it, trying to do the best we can with what we've got. So if you're out there, taking life one day at a time, and occasionally eating cereal for dinner? You're not just surviving—you're thriving.

And tomorrow? Well, tomorrow's another day to keep thriving, one tiny victory at a time.

Printed in Great Britain
by Amazon